D1709996

SPOTLIGHT ON SOCIAL AND EMOTIONAL LEARNING

PLANNING FOR SUCCESS
GOAL SETTING

BRIANNA BATTISTA

PowerKiDS
press.

NEW YORK

Published in 2020 by The Rosen Publishing Group, Inc.
29 East 21st Street, New York, NY 10010

Editor: Rachel Gintner
Designer: Michael Flynn

Photo Credits: Cover Picturenet/Blend Images/Getty Images; cover, pp. 1, 3–6, 8, 10–12, 14, 16, 18, 20, 22–24 (background) TairA/Shutterstock.com; p. 4 lassedesignen/Shutterstock.com; p. 5 NASA/Roger Ressmeyer/Corbis/VCG/Getty Images; p. 6 Tiffany Bryant/Shutterstock.com; p. 7 Kekyalyaynen/Shutterstock.com; p. 9 mooinblack/Shutterstock.com; p. 10 Leonard Zhukovsky/Shutterstock.com; p. 11 Jemal Countess/Getty Images; p. 13 Alexxndr/Shutterstock.com; p. 15 Chip Somodevilla/Shutterstock.com; p. 16 Lotus_studio/Shutterstock.com; p. 17 4 PM production/Shutterstock.com; p. 19 Rachel Murray/Getty Images; p. 21 Images Source/Vetta/Getty Images; p. 22 Kaspars Grinvalds/Shutterstock.com.

Cataloging-in-Publication Data

Names: Battista, Brianna.
Title: Planning for success: goal setting / Brianna Battista.
Description: New York : PowerKids Press, 2020. | Series: Spotlight on social and emotional learning | Includes glossary and index.
Identifiers: ISBN 9781725302082 (pbk.) | ISBN 9781725302273 (library bound) | ISBN 9781725302181 (6pack)
Subjects: LCSH: Goal (Psychology)--Juvenile literature. | Emotions--Juvenile literature. | Motivation (Psychology)--Juvenile literature.
Classification: LCC BF505.G6 B38 2020 | DDC 158.1--dc23

Manufactured in the United States of America

CPSIA Compliance Information: Batch #CSPK19. For further information contact Rosen Publishing, New York, New York at 1-800-237-9932.

CONTENTS

CHAPTER ONE

READY TO CHASE YOUR DREAMS?

Do you ever dream of **achieving** something great in the future? Maybe you hope that you'll be an honor roll student this year. Or maybe you'd like to be an astronaut and travel to outer space when you grow up! It can be fun to let your imagination run wild and to dream up different possibilities for your future. But once you feel serious about an idea and you want to make it become real, it's time to set a goal.

Mae Jemison, the first African American woman in space, knew she wanted to be a scientist even when she was a little girl.

A goal is different from simply having a hope or a wish for the future. Goals help us narrow our focus, make a plan, and figure out how to stick to our vision. Learning how to set goals is an important skill you need to make your dreams happen. Goals are the stepping-stones we take toward our dreams!

CHAPTER TWO

CHOOSING A GOAL

What's the best way to get started when choosing a goal? First, think of something you'd like to do. Have an idea in mind? Great! If not, a good place to begin is with some activities you already spend time on. The second step is to make sure the goal is **specific**. The more specific a goal is, the better you'll be able to create steps that will help you work toward achieving it.

A specific goal usually has a deadline, or a due date, and a way to measure your success. For example, if you want to win a spelling bee, you would find out exactly when the next contest is happening so you have a clear deadline. One way you can measure your **progress** is by counting the number of words you learn along the way.

It's time to pick a goal! What do you want to achieve? Try writing your thoughts down to help you get started.

CHAPTER THREE

FIND YOUR "WHY"

After you've picked a goal that feels specific, it's time to look at it a little more closely. Why do you want this goal? It's good to understand why the goal is important to you. If you feel connected to the reason for your goal, you'll want to work harder to make it happen. Having a goal you care about will push you forward!

It's also a good time to start **researching** more about your goal. It's possible that the goal can help other people in a way you aren't even aware of. All this **information** helps add importance to your goal.

Once you've found your "why," write it in large letters on a piece of paper. Put it in a place where you'll see it every day. Again, the shorter and more specific the goal, the better!

Let's pretend that one of your goals is to run a race. There may be races in your community that help raise money for important causes and charities. Maybe there's a cause you care about that you can support by running!

CHAPTER FOUR

WHO CAME BEFORE YOU?

Chances are, someone else before you has wanted to achieve a similar goal to your own. Who were the people in the past who thought like you? It's up to you to research and find out. If someone has already done what you want to do or achieved something similar, then they've created a path for you to follow! You can see what helped them succeed.

Professional tennis player Nenad Zimonjic signs autographs for fans after practice.

The sky's the limit. Thomas Suarez is shown here accepting an award for his work on smartphone **apps**. He launched his first app when he was 9 years old!

You can also see what other people may have tried that didn't work for them. That's valuable information that you can base your strategy, or plan, on. You don't have to start from scratch and think of everything all by yourself. It's important that we learn from the people who came before us. We can follow the lead of other successful goal setters! After all, you may have a lot in common, and sometimes history repeats itself!

CHAPTER FIVE

BREAK IT DOWN!

It can feel **overwhelming** when you're trying to learn something new. The trick is to take your big goal and break it down into smaller steps. Make sure you can do these steps comfortably or at the skill level you're at now. Ask yourself, what can you take action on and practice doing right now?

It helps to work backward, too. For example, what do you need to do to win a spelling bee? You need to know how to spell a lot of words. How can you learn more words? One idea is to make a list of **difficult** words and write each one down on paper five times a day.

When you plan this way, your list of words should grow in no time! Use this practice to break down each challenge you face toward meeting your goal.

When setting a goal, recording your steps in a chart, such as the one shown on page 13, is very helpful! Read through the example, then go and create your own.

GOAL:
CHAMPION SPELLER!

CHALLENGE 1: LEARN MORE WORDS	CHALLENGE 2: MANAGE STAGE FRIGHT	CHALLENGE 3: SPELL OUT LOUD
PRACTICE WRITING OUT DIFFICULT WORDS 30 MINUTES A DAY	JOIN A PUBLIC SPEAKING GROUP OR CLUB	MAKE FLASHCARDS OF TRICKY WORDS, PRACTICE SPELLING THEM OUT LOUD
ADD NEW WORDS EVERY WEEK	GO TO MEETINGS REGULARLY AND TAKE PART	ASK AN ADULT OR FRIEND TO QUIZ YOU ONCE A WEEK

CHAPTER SIX

THE MASTER PLAN

Now that you've written down all the major steps that you'll need to take to reach your goal, it's time to form a master plan. This plan will include all those steps along with some smaller goals along the way. A calendar might come in handy here! If your goal is to practice an activity for 30 minutes a day, you can **schedule** it on your calendar each day at a certain time, say, from 7 to 7:30 p.m. In a few weeks, schedule a time to test how far you've come. The goal against which you test yourself is called a benchmark.

It's also important to be honest with yourself about the time you have. Depending on your schedule, it might be wiser to plan to practice for 15 minutes each day. Try to shoot for something you know you can stick to.

Karthik Nemmani, shown here, was the Scripps National Spelling Bee champion in 2018. Leading up to the bee, he studied four hours a day—sometimes more!

CHAPTER SEVEN

BUDDY SYSTEM

You might've thought of the idea for your goal on your own, but you don't have to work on it alone. For example, practicing spelling out loud can be tricky if you don't have a partner to quiz you. There might be a computer game or phone app that you can use. But it's also fun to use your goal as the reason to get together with a friend and practice!

Another way you can get help is to ask for **feedback**. This might make sense if you're learning a new skill, such as drawing or cooking. Receiving feedback can be difficult, but just remember that you're a beginner. When someone has a **negative** comment, it can actually be more helpful than positive comments. Feedback helps you learn and grow to be even better at something.

> If your goal is to learn how to make five different desserts, you'll probably be able to find some friends to taste them for you!

CHAPTER EIGHT

FEELING FRUSTRATED

How long will it take to set, work toward, and reach your goal? The good news is that goals won't take forever to achieve when you're following your master plan. Day by day, you can make progress and get closer. It's natural to feel **frustrated** along the way—learning a new skill takes time, and some things are easier to learn than others.

Try writing down how you're feeling in a journal and **express** the emotions that are coming to mind. No matter what happens, don't give up! If your master plan feels too difficult, you might need to make changes. You need time to relax, too! Whatever your goal may be, if you think about it and work toward it every day, you're becoming better at something that's important to you. Try to keep the bigger picture in mind.

It can also help to find some new inspiration when you feel frustrated. Gitanjali Rao, shown here, created a device to test how safe drinking water is when she was 11.

CHAPTER NINE

TRY, TRY AGAIN

It's very likely that you'll face some **obstacles** when trying to achieve your goal. Perhaps when the time comes for you to practice, you're tired from school. Or maybe your friend wants to see a movie with you when you should be working on your goal. Even finding it difficult to focus is an obstacle!

Try to be patient and understanding with yourself. You might need a break if your schedule has felt very demanding, or challenging. You don't want to burn out, which is when you work yourself too hard and lose energy. Just remember, you can be open to changes. Reschedule your practice time, or make sure to get back on track the next day. The reward of accomplishing a goal is sweet, but there's a lot of work that needs to happen for you to get there.

It's important to make time for fun! Everyone needs space in their life for relaxation and time with the people they love.

CHAPTER TEN

STILL IN TRAINING

The first time you set a goal that's important to you, it can feel overwhelming. You might feel like you'll never get there. But fear not—the more you set goals, the better you'll get at achieving what you set out to do. You're still a goal setter in training! No one is a master at anything when they're first starting out.

The more you work, the more you'll learn. Your **confidence** will grow in your ability to break down tasks and find a path to reach your goals. Setting goals is a powerful skill to have and one that will come in handy throughout your entire life. After all, you can set goals whether you're young or old!

Still looking for that first goal? Maybe a start could be getting better at goal setting!

Sometimes it takes courage to name your goals and to chase them with everything you've got! Just know that if you put yourself out there and put in the work, you will likely succeed again and again.

GLOSSARY

achieve (uh-CHEEV) To get by effort.

app (APP) Short for application, a program that performs a task for which a smartphone or computer is used.

confidence (KAHN-fuh-dens) A feeling of trust or belief.

difficult (DIH-fih-kuhlt) Hard to do, make, or carry out.

express (ik-SPRES) To communicate what you're thinking or feeling.

feedback (FEED-bak) Helpful information that someone gives to show what can be improved.

frustrated (fruh-STRAY-tihd) Feeling angered or let down.

information (ihn-fuhr-MAY-suhn) Knowledge or facts about something.

negative (NEH-guh-tiv) Harmful or bad, also unwanted.

obstacle (AHB-stuh-kuhl) Something that stops forward movement or progress.

overwhelming (oh-vuhr-WELL-ming) Overpowering in thought or feeling.

progress (PRAH gruhs) Movement toward a goal.

research (ree-SUHRCH) Careful study to find new knowledge.

schedule (SKEH-jool) A list of times when certain events will happen.

specific (spih-SIH-fik) Clearly and exactly presented or stated.

INDEX

PRIMARY SOURCE LIST

Page 5
Mae Jemison in Spacelab. Photograph. NASA, Roger Ressmeyer, Corbis, and VCG. Getty Images.

Page 11
Thomas Suarez at the Tribeca Disruptive Innovation Awards. Photograph. Jemal Countess. April 27, 2012. Getty Images.

Page 15
Karthik Nemmani winning the National Spelling Bee. Photograph. Chip Somodevilla. May 31, 2018. Getty Images.

WEBSITES